A NOT-SO-EASY TARGET

Practical Tips for Protecting and Equipping Your Child

Matthew Dermody

A Not-So-Easy Target:
Practical Tips for Protecting and Equipping Your Child

Other Published Works by Matthew Dermody

Books:
Hidden Success: A Comprehensive Guide to Ghillie Suit Construction
Appear to Vanish: Stealth Concepts for Effective Camouflage and Concealment
Gray Man: Camouflage for Crowds, Cities, and Civil Crisis
Gray Woman: A Woman's Guide to Gray Man Tactics (e-book)
Hidden in Plain Sight: A Prepper's Guide to Hiding, Discovering, and Scavenging Diversion Safes and Caches
Conversational Camouflage: Oratory Discretion and Pretexting for Behavior Concealment
Situational Sense: Basic Threat Detection Using Situational Awareness and Common Sense
Going Gray: The Urban Concealment and Survival Anthology

ACKNOWLEDGEMENTS

No acknowledgement section would be complete without the inclusion of my wonderful wife and our twin girls. Their faithful support and encouragement are essential to my writing success. I love you very much.

DISCLAIMER

INTRODUCTION

Most parents desire to protect their children. Our existence on the planet would be considerably shorter if our parents and all the many others before them believed the opposite were true. There are many things on the planet threatening our daily existence and trying to mitigate or reduce our own exposure as well as that of our children is important.

We have a moral obligation as parents to be the protector of our children. We cannot ambivalently or idly abstain from our duties as parents. As we have grown increasingly aware of the many dangers lurking and looking to devour our children, we sometimes find it overwhelming to know where to start. Furthermore, we must balance our actions, so they are not overly paranoid or overly permissive.

My children are now entering young adulthood. The time has flown by. My wife and I have excelled in some areas and failed in others. We are not perfect, nor do we pretend to be. But, regardless of successes or setbacks, we press on to diligently and faithfully steward and nurture our girls. We purposely avoid the speaking the phrase "raising children", as we believe (to varying degrees) you get what you say. Therefore, "children" tend to be the net result. Instead, we focus on equipping our children to find and follow a pathway into reasoned, responsible adulthood.

It's no surprise that several of the last few generations have been accused of being self-absorbed, entitled brats. Some of that is the fault of the child, but the bulk of the causation falls directly upon the parents and their lack of quality parenting decisions and choices.[1] Many parents have lost the ability or desire to tell their children, "No." In doing so, we as a society, have failed to realistically prepare children for inevitable disappointments and setbacks that they will encounter throughout life. We also tend to forget that the experimentation we dabbled in during our youth has grown more prolific, more permissive, and more perilous. Items considered contraband back when I was a teen took more effort to obtain. Illicit drugs are certainly more potent and addictive. Age restricted items are often purchased online and delivered to a friend's address using a credit or debit card. Pornography is accessible with an internet connection and a couple of mouse clicks.

Keeping our children safe requires a multi-faceted approach. We must provide them with solid explanations and expectations regarding right and wrong. We must provide meaningful and acceptable alternative activities to keep them from exploring unacceptable ones. We then must provide appropriate rewards and actionable consequences. Then we must provide advice and counsel to correct mistakes or keep them along the course trajectory into adulthood. It sometimes is not an easy job. It is my hope that the suggestions offered within this guide will serve to help set some parenting goals or reinforce the ones you have already set.

These suggestions are not dependent upon the skill level or knowledge of the parent. The parent would obviously benefit from the suggestions as well, but it's unrealistic to assume that most parents would be proficient in everything listed in this book. It is the responsibility of the parent to determine their own skill level and take it upon themselves to provide the training and instruction to their child or enroll them into classes. These are not skills providing something to pass the time away. They are life skills intended to help the child mature into productive adulthood with success and confidence. For example, enrolling your child in the Scouts or taking wilderness survival courses will often teach or expound upon several of the proposed tips suggested throughout this book.

It is also important to remember where it says, "Teach your child..." it doesn't automatically mean that *you* have to teach them. As parents, we are our children's first teacher. It is our responsibility, but it doesn't mean we have to do it alone. Nor does it mean we are required to present something recklessly or lacking the proper knowledge of a subject. There are suggestions within this book in which I'm not qualified or possess the proper knowledge and skills to teach my children. That's okay. Now it means there is a skill that I can learn at the same time, allowing my children to see my need and desire to continue learning throughout life. It also provides additional time to bond with your child and maintain that bond when they enter young adulthood.

Furthermore, these suggestions are not dependent upon the ability of the child, but rather on where the parent feels the child is ready, based on responsibility and maturity. There are the certain exceptions for those children with physical and developmental limitations. A consultation with the family doctor is recommended prior to commencing any of the listed physical activity suggestions. The goal is to have a well-rounded, prepared child; but not at the expense of overwhelming them with life situations or knowledge they aren't emotionally ready to address. There are topics mentioned that are difficult and uncomfortable to discuss with a child. Only the parent can know how ready their child is to bring those topics to light or how in-depth the parent wants to be in their discussion.

This book will be at odds with some of what is generally regarded now as child safety. This is not intended for the parent who wishes to shield their child from the realities of cuts, scrapes, and bruises. Nor is it for the parent who demands that their personal safety and that of their child is the sole responsibility of the state or is subject to governmental restriction or intervention. It is also not for the timid or the passive, nor is for parents who have decidedly abandoned the truth that life is hard, requires effort, and there are no trophies for just showing up.

There is a lot of beauty in our world that children should be able to discover, observe, and enjoy. The harsh reality is there are ugly, wretched things present in the world with the potential of negating the ability to participate in the former. This information is not intended to frighten, but to inform and prepare your child for adulthood. Will your child have to use every skill they learn? Maybe, maybe not. It is better to have a skill or a tool and not need it, than to need it and not have it.

This book was difficult to write in the sense that the world can no longer be observed from within a bubble of naivety. It requires an acknowledgement that the evil and ugliness in this world forces us to change our perception of the world and how we function within society because of its existence. The very content, based on the subject matter and the countless scenarios that put our children at risk, are unpleasant to think about and discuss. They are the things of every parent's nightmare. It has forced me to look upon some of that ugliness and the consequences in an effort to keep my children from becoming both victims and statistics.

There are many potential dangers and pitfalls awaiting our children throughout their life. It is our responsibility to prepare and train them to acknowledge, confront, and deal with adversity and hardships as they enter into adulthood. The content and the application of the advice given herein, along with the necessary parental guidance and involvement, will help them reach adulthood physically, mentally, and emotionally prepared.

The intent of this book is just what is alluded to in the title: It provides tips, advice, and suggestions. It is not an in-depth study of everything proposed. This is because I don't know you, your skill level, your knowledge level, or the specific needs of your child. There will be those who find the say it's too protective, too paranoid, and too restrictive. Still others will claim it lacking more of the desired "how-to" for implementation. My justification is that my children are alive, safe, and both physically and emotionally healthy because my wife and I have implemented the presented material, not in spite of it. It is my endeavor and hope that your child or children will be equally safe.

[1]https://www.thriveglobal.com/stories/21155-7-damaging-parenting-behaviors-that-keep-children-from-growing-into-leaders

Teach your child about the existence of evil.

Photo courtesy of www.pixabay.com

Evil is present in the world and it *IS* out there, everywhere. One need not look any further than the nightly news to see the graphic evidence. Some of it is brazen and flaunted openly. However, most of what is diabolically malevolent and wicked is usually hidden from plain view. Pure evil cannot flourish and grow in places where the rule of law is present and respected.

It is like a fungus. It does not produce its harvest in open fields, bathed in sunlight and soil teeming with nutrients. It is like a mushroom, grown in darkness and multiplying in an abundance of excrement.

It was once said, "Evil exists only when good men choose to do nothing." Part of that nothing includes ignoring or denying the existence of evil and evildoers. Age appropriate shielding is necessary to a certain degree and all conversations with your child must be held at a comprehension level necessary for them to understand the information. The key component in the last sentence is conversation.

In the 21st century, we have lost the fine art of communication. We've relinquished our ability to effectively communicate in person; deferring what little skill we may have to the realms of technology. Things like vocal tone, inflection, and body language are either non-existent or now require an emoji for the appropriate emphasis. It is for this very reason parents must engage their children in direct, intentional conversation.

Assure them of the existence of good.

Photo courtesy of www.pixabay.com

Assuring your child of the existence of good is the sole responsibility of the parent. If we know what is evil, doing the opposite should be acceptable in society. Historically, religion has been the standard by which many concepts of good and evil are distinguished. Regardless of the religious beliefs one ascribes to, in order to keep a healthy balance and perspective, we must ensure that our children know that there are good things and good people on this earth.

This all begins in the home and parents have the responsibility to provide a safe and stable environment (to the best of their ability) for their children. As parents, we should strive to be our child's first and best example of goodness, unconditional love, and trust. It is a tremendous responsibility and it is extremely tough to do 24 hours a day, seven days a week, 365 days a year. Anyone who says it is easy is a liar or they are doing it wrong. I have yet to meet a parent that can balance their own life perfectly and shield their child from all of the stressors faced as an adult.

While we are not perfect and prone to make mistakes, our children know there are avenues for forgiveness when those mistakes are made, allowing corrections to be made in words and action. This is the example we use to remind our children of the nature and qualities of good people.

Teach your child how to read and write.

Photo courtesy of www.pixabay.com

If there is one skill that is the lynchpin to all other learned life skills, it is reading and writing. The earlier you can start your child's journey into the wonderful and endless world of reading, the better. We started reading to our girls very early, and as a result, we now have two girls starting their teen years as voracious readers who both read at grade levels higher than their current enrollment.

In addition to fostering this valuable skill, it has also developed a secondary passion for creative writing and storytelling. When a child learns to read, it unlocks a door into a world of countless subjects of potential interest to the child. Their use of imagination transports them further and faster than they can travel by any other means. In our family's case, it has inspired both of our girls to participate in the writing process. One loves to develop plots and characters while the other prefers the creative freedom of illustrating her sister's stories.

The other positive aspect reading gives to each child is its freedom to learn about any subject in which they have an interest. As parents, despite our children's biased tendency to exaggerate our aptitude and intelligence, we don't know everything. As such, we can easily keep our egos in check by telling our children when we don't know a particular answer or how to answer their questions. However, this is where we sometimes fail as parents. We can sometimes brush away our children's natural curiosity by giving them the "I don't know" answer.

By offering them the avenues to seek out the answers through reading, they learn through repetition how to investigate their desired level of research into a subject. Reading is a basic investigative tool used to address problems and discovering potential solutions, so fostering this skill has many advantages and rewards.

Writing skills fall in nicely as well. They promote memory retention and communication skills. It is hard to find people who can successfully retain information only having read the source material once. Studying and writing notes is one way to ensure the information stays in our memory longer. The information your children retain may save their life.

Teach your child how to cook and prepare food.

Photo courtesy of www.pixabay.com

Teaching your child how to cook and assisting during meal preparation provides a great many benefits. First, it allows the child to participate and positively contribute to the family. Cooking teaches problem solving, temperature, fractions, conversions, dry and liquid measurement, chemistry, diet, and human physiology without the parent being overwhelmed by the role of a schoolteacher. It also teaches responsibility and a certain level of self-reliance, in which a child learns that he or she can provide some of their basic dietary needs.

Cooking and baking provides a child with a sense of accomplishment. The added bonus of eating their culinary creations also opens the door for the child to expand his or her palate and discover new foods. The child will also learn about nutrition, ingredients, food safety, and sanitation.

The best part from a parent's perspective is it further reinforces utensil safety, sanitation, and cleaning up. While cleaning up is never as much fun as measuring and mixing ingredients, it is still part of the cooking/baking process. Children who end up just doing the clean up and clearing the table after dinner are much more likely to complain about the task. They see a mess that they didn't directly take part in creating. As parents, we are quick to point out and instruct our children if the child made the mess, he or she is responsible for the clean up.

While it should never be our sole intention that a child be able to fend for itself, it does lessen the anxiety of both parent and child when the child can prepare a snack or meal safely and correctly. Sandwiches are simple enough and require enough ingredients and utensils in the preparation to learn some of the aforementioned concepts. As the child grows older, more complex, multiple-step recipes can be introduced to reinforce the sequences of preparation as well as several dishes finishing the baking/cooking process at the same time for mealtimes.

Teach your child code words to use when encountering strangers.

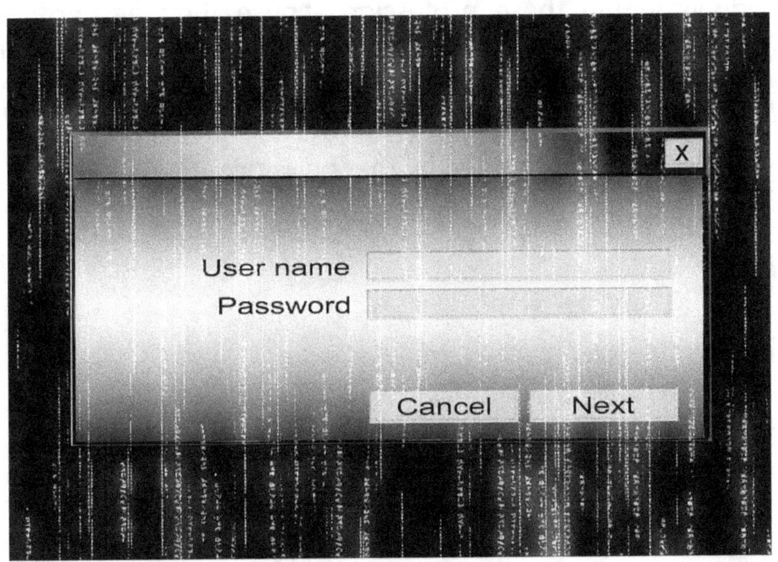

Photo courtesy of www.pixabay.com

This tactic is what my wife and I decided upon rather than instructing our children to yell, "Stranger Danger!" Most child abductions occur when a perpetrator either pretends to be or is a family friend or a distant family relative whom the child may not be able to identify visually.

My wife and I also taught our children early regarding the difference between friends, acquaintances, and strangers. Any person who approached our children claiming to act on our behalf or on our instructions needed to know our family password. If they did not know the password, the girls either stayed put or were to proceed immediately to a place of safety.

This teaches the child the importance of earning trust and to whom trust should be granted. Years ago, it was assumed that police, doctors, and members of the clergy were deemed trustworthy. Today, we find little comfort when we learn of individuals within these professions abuse their authority and destroy the level of trust bestowed upon them. It is even less comforting to their victims. As a result, we have little alternative but to treat everyone we do not know reasonable suspicion; even if it means they are offended by that decision.

Use games to teach situational awareness to your child.

Photo courtesy of www.pixabay.com

I briefly touched upon the subject of situational awareness in two of my previous books, *Gray Man* and *Situational Sense.* In both books, I explained a couple of the games I used to teach my children about the concept of being mindful of one's surroundings. Smaller children can learn this concept starting with shapes and colors once their vocabulary develops. Games like "Find Something Blue" or "Find Circles" instantly begin developing a child's ability to discern and analyze the world around them.

While there are many interactive television shows and apps that promote this concept to a certain degree, screen time should be avoided. There is plenty of research evidence describing the negative side effects of prolonged time spent in front of the television or the computer screen. In addition, it reinforces the necessary bonding between parent and child.

It is considerably better to engage your child's cognitive learning through interacting with the real, tangible world. Staring at a monitor or touch-screen for hours on end creates a tunnel vision effect in which the child shuts out or shuts down other sensory input. How often have you called your child's name announcing dinner, only to have to repeat yourself several times because the child is so heavily involved in a video game or television program that all other audio stimuli is not heard or ignored as a "distraction?"

This is the same type of distraction and many others like it that end up putting people into dangerous situations that could have been avoided when they are not paying attention to their surroundings. It is a bad habit to establish in adults and children.

Keep footprint records of your child's footwear.

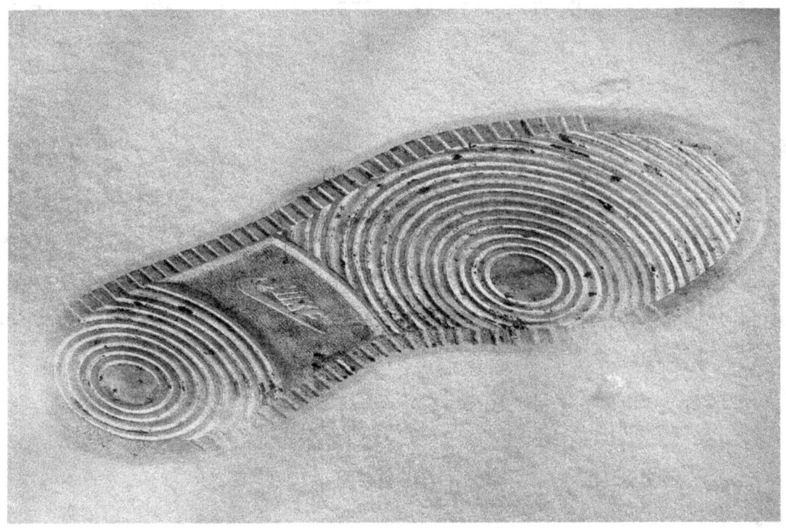

Photo courtesy of www.pixabay.com

I have several mentors and colleagues who are experienced mantrackers, both from military/police and from search and rescue (SAR) backgrounds. Their abilities are honed through constant training, or "dirt time". Mantracking is the disciplined act of observing and following a set of footprints to determine the direction travelled by a lost individual or a person who is actively fleeing apprehension/prior custody in an effort to locate and recover that individual.

There have been many tragic tales of children lost in the woods, only to find a lifeless body days or weeks later. There are also a great number of successful recoveries. Reuniting children with loved ones are the result of mantrackers employing their skills to aid in location and recovery.

One thing that often aids mantrackers in search and rescue operations is footprints. Footprints allow mantrackers to identify the lost individual by analyzing their gait, foot size, tread pattern, etc. Experienced mantrackers can even determine behaviors and intentions based upon evidence and clues left within a footprint.

By taking this simple step (pun intended), trackers can immediately begin their search with that crucial information in hand. Some tracking apps and databases have large catalogs of stored sole imprints from some shoe manufacturers. So even if you do not have a photo of your child's shoeprint, the data may be found through the make and model of the shoe. However, one cannot rely on the databases or apps to have every design stored in the app or updated regularly. It is better to have a photo. Be sure to take a photo every time the child receives a new pair of shoes.

Keep and carry recent photos of your child.

Photo courtesy of www.pixabay.com

This is one of the easiest things to help you protect your child. Almost everyone owns a mobile phone nowadays. There should be no excuse for a parent not to have their child's photo. In the unfortunate event involving the abduction of a child or the child wanders off at a shopping mall, having a current picture of your child to aid searchers and the police is crucial.

Smartphones make this very easy and before heading out to places where there are large numbers of people present, snap a quick photo of your child. This provides you with the most recent picture to describe your child to relevant personnel should the unthinkable happen.

I was once employed as a security guard in a large shopping center. It never failed during the Christmas season, almost every day I was assigned on duty; we would have a report of a missing/separated child. While our recovery rate while I was actively employed there was 100%, it can be the most stressful five to thirty minutes in a shift. We were always able to review video footage faster when we had accurate descriptions and last known locations.

The event usually unfolds the same way with the parent stating, "I just turned away for a minute, and he/she was gone." I was astonished when there were times when the parent or grandparent could not recall what the child was wearing. Part of that memory lapse could be factored as stress-induced. Had the parent or grandparent taken a picture of the child before starting their shopping excursion, we wouldn't have had to rely on poor and/or inaccurate descriptions.

Teach your children to memorize important phone numbers and addresses.

Photo courtesy of www.pixabay.com

In as much as the smartphone has made taking and storing pictures easier, it has also done this to telephone numbers; often detrimentally. Many people cannot remember their or their spouse's mobile numbers and many people no longer maintain a traditional landline telephone. I am among the guilty, as I often have to look up my wife's phone number, but I still can recall from memory my childhood phone number. It was drilled into my mind as a necessity that I doubt I will ever forget it.

Teaching your child to memorize important phone numbers and addresses give them an automatic help line to a parent, family friend, or emergency services; even if they forget, lose, or don't own a mobile phone. When children are younger, they may have difficulty memorizing numbers or having the ability to match the person to the correct number.

This can be remedied by laminating a piece of paper with the most important numbers and placing it in a zippered pocket of their backpack. This is not a foolproof solution, as these can be lost or accidentally laundered if the child decides to carry the list in a trouser pocket.

Use and enforce curfews with your child.

Photo courtesy of www.pixabay.com

As your child gets older, he or she will desire more personal freedom to make his or her own choices. Approaching the legally recognized age of adulthood, children will naturally want to test and expand boundaries.

While no one likes it when an imposed curfew forces the cancellation or curtailing of planned activities, most people like the comfort and predictability of having a set time to be expected. Any deviation extending past the set time tends to invoke slight dread or panic in an adult.

When curfews are initially set, there should be no allowances made for tardiness. Strictness is the key to ensure the child adheres to the expectations. After a determined length of time of consistent obedience to the curfew has elapsed, a later curfew can be set.

There may be times when delays occur, but these should be very infrequent and should require immediate contact from the child or the designated chaperone. As a parent, you can demand as much information necessary to set your mind at ease and realistically set an expected time of arrival based upon the prevailing conditions.

If your child is still exhibiting difficulty obeying household rules like cleaning up or uses disrespectful language/tones and body language when communicating for whatever reason, I would suggest your child isn't ready for the responsibilities associated with curfews, especially those set after daylight hours.

Teach your child to travel in pairs or groups whenever possible.

Photo courtesy of www.pixabay.com

In today's day and age, it is simply unwise to travel anywhere alone. In most cases, there is safety in numbers. However, more people can mean more witnesses in the minds of those with criminal intentions.

Traveling with a companion can potentially reduce the probability of being targeted. It also provides a person who can seek help if the other becomes ill or injured. Our daughters seldom, if ever, go anywhere without each other, with the exception of their individual training programs. There again, they have fellow classmates who then fulfill the role of companion.

This concept is not strictly for children. The military, especially the Army and Marine Corps focus on and promote the use of implementing a "battle buddy." This means, whether a soldier or Marine is out on a patrol or out on liberty, someone is watching their back. It is harder to abduct two people instead of one. A buddy can be a secondary (or maybe the only) voice of reason in a less than ideal situation. A buddy can render aid or seek help if you are unable to help yourself.

This does not mean that one is necessarily out of danger. Larger crowds are favorite targets of terrorists and mass shooters looking to guarantee the possibility of large body counts and casualties. However, it does reduce isolated and targeted attacks against the lone individual in many cases.

Teach your child to establish and adhere to relationship boundaries.

Photo courtesy of www.pixabay.com

Children, as well as adults, need set boundaries in life to establish proper behavior and relationships in society. They also need to know and understand the rules and view boundaries from the correct perspective. In the photo above, the sport of tennis is one of many sports incorporating the use of boundaries. One can see clearly the ball coming partially to rest on an established boundary line. The question then becomes, from what angle, side, or perspective is this photo taken? By answering this question, we can determine whether the ball is in the field of "play" or just outside the boundary and violating the established rules. If the field of play is to the left, the ball is out of bounds, but if the playing field is to the right, it is fair and legitimate according to the rules.

Establishing boundaries with children helps them to understand and navigate what is safe and unsafe. By committing to using boundaries, children will have the added benefits of love, safety, and stability; making them better equipped when someone clearly steps "out of bounds" in the conduct shown to them by others.

Here again, if your child is lacking in some of the basics mentioned back in Chapter 10 regarding curfews, you, as a parent, have some foundational work to establish or reestablish to ensure your child is going to survive adolescence and move into adulthood successfully.

Teach your child the basics of minor automobile repairs.

Photo courtesy of www.pixabay.com

Modern technological advances in today's vehicles make it almost impossible for the average owner to perform his or her own vehicle repairs and regular maintenance. However, teaching your driving age teenager how to check and fill operating fluids such as engine oil, windshield washer fluid, and antifreeze is a good way to reduce the chances of vehicle failure.

This, by no means, requires your child unrealistically to be an ASE-certified vehicle mechanic, but having some basic knowledge allows them to notify a parent of potential problems with a vehicle before they become worse.

Teaching your teen how to identify warning indicators on the instrument panel is both necessary for safe vehicle operation as well as identifying potential problems requiring immediate service repairs.

Other checks include tire pressure and visual inspections of the braking system, exhaust system, and suspension. Being able to recognize obvious and subtle wear on essential mechanical parts can reduce the chances of becoming stranded on the side of the road where there is limited or no immediate assistance.

It's unfortunate in today's society that most people more hesitant to help a stranger with vehicle trouble. It does not help that rapists, serial killers, and kidnappers have used this tactic to lure unsuspecting victims. In these situations, rather than getting out of the vehicle and assisting, ask if the stranded person(s) need you to call the police, roadside assistance, or a towing service.

Enroll your child in skill-based education platforms.

Photo courtesy of www.pixabay.com

Not every parent is comfortable in the great outdoors and many cannot teach certain life skills that will aid their child in the future. However, there are organizations, clubs, and after school programs specifically designed to teach children these necessary life skills. Many of the chapter headings in this book are skills taught by both the Boy Scouts and Girl Scouts of America.

While I am at odds with some of the current philosophies and social policies enacted by both organizations, their impact on earlier generations is undeniable. The skills presented by Scout leaders and subject matter experts, along with the attainment of goals through the awarding of merit badges contributed to high levels of enrollment into the programs. The hopes of earning the title of Eagle Scout or the Girl Scout Gold Award, gives both boys and girls the motivation and perseverance to excel and earn a title that would mean something to them and be held in high esteem by others.

Other organizations that offer various programs and useful life skills are local YMCA centers and 4-H clubs. My love for the outdoors is directly connected to the couple of years I spent in the Ranger Rick program that was offered. Certain communities may have an independent vocational or a community center that offers classes or seminars on a regular basis.

Enroll your child in self-defense classes.

Photo courtesy of www.pixabay.com

Self-defense training is particularly adept at helping children develop self-esteem and confidence, as well as discipline and respect. It is a strong, proactive deterrent towards bullying and teaches self-control.

I spent a good portion of my adolescence angry at the world and the people whom I allowed to make it miserable, based upon my own flawed perceptions. Half way through junior high, I had enough and sought out how to deal with the constant bullying I endured. My dad was my first instructor who taught me basic self-defense.   While I was never enrolled in any formal martial arts classes, the additional discipline from another adult other than my parents may have helped.

Looking back on those days made me realize as a parent that this was a path I did not want my children to travel ill prepared.   I want them to be assertive, confident, and have enough self-respect to stand up for themselves if Mom and Dad cannot be there to intervene.

I would steer clear of sport-based martial arts and focus on instruction that is more combatives-based which should include teaching on mindset and preparedness, rather than just learning how to block, strike, and kick. I believe children exposed to too many rules in sports martial arts will not properly engage a threat, will hesitate for a "Fight!" command, or simply will not execute effective techniques because a particular technique is deemed illegal or unfair within a sporting or sportsmanship context.

Teach your child firearm safety and shooting skills.

Photo courtesy of www.pixabay.com

This suggestion will probably raise some controversy among some parents, but it has proven to be an invaluable skill when dangerous situations are presented. While it is true that there are many accidental shootings involving children, most are the result of unsupervised curiosity and improperly stored firearms. Teaching your child proper and safe firearm handling will correct a majority of these incidents. First, it sets the boundaries and conditions in which the child is allowed to handle the firearm. Second, familiarity reduces curiosity.

My father was a police officer so there was always a loaded firearm in the house. He made it clear to us that firearms were to be considered loaded at all times. They were not to be touched without him present and having been cleared by him prior to any of us children touching any firearm. He went on to explain safe handling practices while letting us inspect it, point the weapon in a safe direction, dry-fire the weapon, and ask questions about how the weapon functions.

This type of introduction to firearms curbed any curiosity I had and because my father allowed my brothers and me to participate in cleaning, assembly and disassembly, as well as various stages of the reloading process, we gained a desire to learn more with each encounter.

My reasoning for adding this tip is to suggest the required marksmanship skills to hunt safely and ethically, as a means for a responsible young person to learn about wildlife conservation practices in addition to having the ability to put food on the table. Junior shooting leagues and hunting serves as a bridge for proper gun safety and handling while still attaining marksmanship skills. As the child enters into adulthood and reaches the legal age to lawfully purchase and carry a firearm, they themselves can then choose whether they wish to do so.

Teach your child about improvised weapons.

Photo courtesy of www.pixabay.com

A child's imagination can take the simplest object and magically transform it into a toy. Likewise, as the child grows, circumstances may arise when the child needs access to a proverbial equalizer to an encountered threat. This doesn't mean automatically that the object is strictly offensive in its use or application. The object could be something that purely serves as a defensive tool. For example, a trash can lid does not have any sharp edges, but its mass is large enough to use as a defensive shield, protecting the child from knife attacks or blunt force trauma.

While it's true, most children are not the target of direct assaults and attacks. As such, legislators acting in good faith, prohibit the use of certain weapons due to the level of responsibility and maturity of most children. While this may be true from a statistical or numbers viewpoint, that number is not zero, unfortunately.

When children are attacked and preyed upon by adults or older children, they are often overpowered by the physical size and strength of the attacker. As such, children are at a distinct disadvantage when it comes to the self-defense tools available to them to carry, both practically and legally. If it were not for the predatory behaviors of adults, the lack of severe punishment under the law, and the eventual release of a good portion of convicted sex offenders into public, this topic would not need discussion.

The sad and horrifying fact remains that released predators and those who have not been apprehended before (or yet) continue to prey upon children, often luring them away or brazenly abducting them. In order to give your child the best defense in a potential attack, teaching them how to recognize and utilize available tools and objects to thwart attacks is a skill worth equipping your child.

Teach your child the basics of first aid.

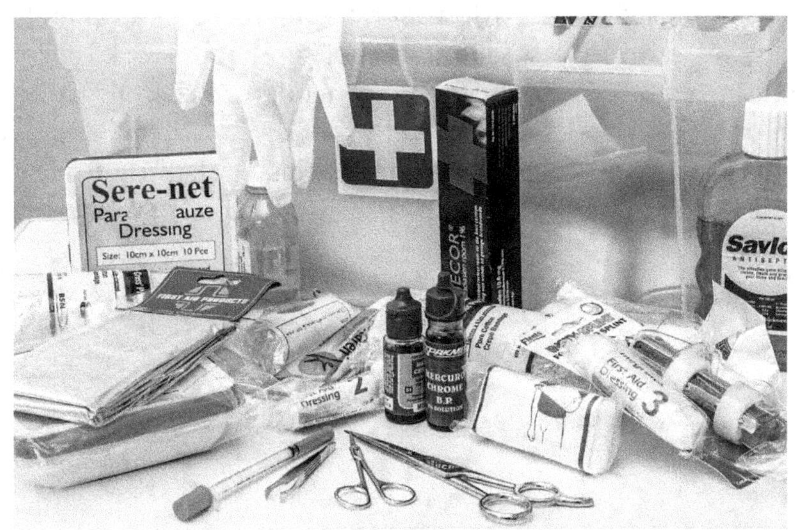

Photo courtesy of www.pixabay.com

Children seem to have a built-in knack for getting hurt. It is often a powerful learning tool in the school of hard knocks and the tutor known as experience is sometimes unmerciful. This is not only a good practice for their safety, but also yours as their parent.

For a child, nothing can be as frightening and disturbing as seeing one of their parents hurt or seriously injured. A portion of that fright is connected to the inability to help. While every child is different and some may not be able to cope with some of the aspects of treating a major trauma injury, they can help with cleaning and bandaging minor wounds, applying heat/cold packs, and administering certain medications. Children who have severe allergic or medical conditions may be knowledgeable regarding the self-administration of anaphylactic or diabetic treatments, including injections.

As children grow and take on more adult responsibilities, having them learn how to properly administer CPR, immobilize limbs and extremities, and treat victims for shock becomes increasingly useful. This is especially needed when children travel on hiking or biking excursions with friends or with an adult who becomes injured. I cannot emphasize this enough that this type of training should only be taught and facilitated by certified first-aid instructors.

Background check your child's friends *and* their parents.

Photo courtesy of www.pixabay.com

Despite the chapter title, it does not necessarily mean a full on, deep probing check into the history of a person. A good majority of the time, your child will tell you about fellow students and the ones they befriend. They often reveal those whom they don't particularly care for as well.

It's not hard to deduce that some kids come from broken homes or suffer through horrendous abuse, both verbal and physical. As a result of feeling hurt and powerless at home, they exert whatever power they can muster and torment someone weaker as a coping mechanism for their own sense of powerlessness.

Some parents simply are so consumed with their own day-to-day lives and dealing with their own personal demons, they are unaware of their child's behavior. Even worse, they turn a blind eye to it with excuses and denials that the child will somehow "grow" out of it. It's true, the child might. However, along the way, they tend to make life miserable for others that deal with them on a daily basis, from teachers all the way to classmates.

There have been too many horror stories of children being molested and exploited by neighbors and the parents of their friends. As a result, our girls are not allowed to attend or host sleep-overs. For some parents, that may seem harsh and overly paranoid. My wife and I are satisfied with our decision, and thankfully our girls understand and favor the arrangement.

Limit or prohibit your child's access to social media and the Internet.

Photo courtesy of www.pixabay.com

I have seen this post or a paraphrased version of it on countless social media accounts of friends and associates. The post often states how grateful the individual is that the Internet or social media didn't exist when they were children. Most of the time, it is the result of seeing how young people today are cyberbullied and harassed by simple, yet embarrassing mistakes as they attempt to navigate through adolescence. It is unfortunate and heartbreaking to learn of the young people who tragically end their lives through suicide because of the stigma of a life situation that found its way onto a social media platform.

Any social media app that wants access to your phone's camera, microphone, and contacts lists should be used with caution. Any app that features the ability for photos or messages to be deleted automatically after a certain time period elapses are a big red flag. Apps like SnapChat and Tik-Tok come to mind immediately.

There are monitoring apps and internet filtering software available for those wishing to utilize the features they provide. It is completely up to the parents to decide how much and to what extent they want to use these forms of voluntary surveillance methods. They are not foolproof nor are they without some third-party involvement and monitoring. With all types of electronic monitoring, the parents must acknowledge that information collected can also be stored and shared without the express consent of those being monitored.

Explain and teach your child about choices and the proper role of bias.

Photo courtesy of www.pixabay.com

Today's society, with its skewed sense of social justice and virtue signaling, demands zero tolerance of bias and discrimination, regardless of reason, experience, or discretion. The result is we put our children and ourselves at risk strictly for not offending anyone.

As I have mentioned in one of my previous books, *Gray Man*, our choices to segregate or disassociate from different people is merely a form of preemptive conflict resolution. If I have a differing political view, I don't go to a rally or political march favoring an opposing position. Why heap abuse upon myself? Why stir the pot of dissention and deliberately anger someone else with my presence? Why risk making someone agitated to the point of physical violence?

Likewise, I am free to make choices based on personal preferences and beliefs. If I like Coca-Cola better than Pepsi, I can choose. It doesn't mean I hate Pepsi. It also does not mean that I dislike people who like Pepsi. Let's not forget the people who do not like either and prefer Dr. Pepper, Mountain Dew, or some other soft drink.

Bias serves a very important role in keeping us safe while still allowing us to approach and extend boundaries of acquaintances and friendship at our own comfort zones and levels of trust. Many people view biases through a societal lenses rather than ones of personal safety. Society wants to protect groups from bias at the expense of an individual, regardless of the validity for the bias. This usually results in the exposure of some level of hypocrisy. Many people in society talk a good game regarding inclusion and tolerance, but few are likely to hire a child molester as a babysitter.

As children increase their levels of proficiency with critical thinking skills and logic, the need to identify bias and the negative effects it can have in data gathering. By identifying bias, it will aid them in data interpretation and measuring results when conducting experiments and research.

Establish meet-up locations, safe havens, and evacuation routes with your child.

Photo courtesy of www.pixabay.com

Having a solid, workable family contingency plan is essential to the safety of everyone within a particular family unit. These consist of all emergency action plans, including practice drills for fire, hurricanes, and tornadoes.

As the structural integrity and safety of your house can be potentially compromised through natural disaster or home invasion by burglars, you need to have a designated meet-up place or muster point. This could be a neighbor's house or a makeshift shelter located a safe distance from where the danger is located.

The extent of the emergency or danger will dictate the minimum safe distance requirements, but the smaller the child is, the shorter the distance should be. Children are very line-of-sight and earshot oriented, meaning that if they cannot see or hear you, the child becomes upset and may begin to panic.

It is also important to drill and practice these situations on a regular basis. Having appropriate family discussions about what to do in an emergency will hopefully reduce the panic, hesitation, and confusion when dangerous situations present themselves.

The routes and locations do not need to be elaborate or something out of a spy movie. Nor do they need to be remote unless the situation dictates. Planning a safe location in four directions (matching the points of a compass rose) is the best, but families should at least plan a primary and secondary route and location.

Explain the difference between friends and acquaintances.

Photo courtesy of www.pixabay.com

Children need to know what defines a good friend, the characteristics that should be present, and expected behavior of a true friend. They also need to know how to be a good friend and reciprocate it back to the other. Most childhood friendships, if properly maintained, can continue into adulthood. Even though different paths and opportunities may create geographical distance between people, pleasant memories and the kindred spirit of friendship can keep communication lines open.

We taught our children early to develop acquaintances based off the other child's behavior. As each child vets the behavior of the other, each develops stronger bonds of friendship. As we taught our children what society and we viewed as appropriate behaviors, any child not meeting that metric was kept at a greater distance. This also reinforces the earlier suggestion of background checking your child's friends. It puts some of the responsibility for discernment on your child to determine what characteristics constitute a good friend and which ones do not.

This is not to say that attempts to reach out to other children were not made. However, it was a clear guideline if the other child was not receptive and did not reciprocate the kindness; there was no point in trying to establish a friendship if only one child was going to participate in its development.

Teach your child not to scream unless injured or in danger.

Photo courtesy of www.pixabay.com

This particular point is probably the catalyst for why I decided to write this guide. It is important to understand that this is not a discussion about infants. Crying and screaming are the only ways infants know how to get the basic care they need. Toddlers, on the other hand, are a different story.

Children should be taught early that screaming when playfully excited is not necessary. Screaming is very distracting and sets off parents' protective instincts and by letting a child scream when not injured or in danger has the potential to desensitize parents and other adults in the area. While it cannot be helped or contained all the time, parents should make every effort to keep children from producing ear shattering, blood-curdling screams.

The slippery-slope tendency is often to give in to the child's demands in the hopes of calming the child. Unfortunately, children learn the skill of manipulation easily through cause and effect. The child learns that the louder he or she cries, disrupting the atmosphere, the result is he or she receives something in order to stop.

I had a college professor posit this question during one of my criminal justice courses. He asked, "Which age demographic in society is the most violent?" Naturally, most students offered answers 18-25 year olds, others mentioned 30-45 year olds, and so on. However, the answer is 2-4 year olds. The violence they commit rarely produces anything beyond superficial injuries, but it is still non-consensual violence. Toddlers are notorious for attempting to hit, kick, bite, and throw fits of rage when they do not get what they want. Children that receive little or no disciplinary correction carry that behavior into adulthood where it often manifests with greater consequence and effects.

Teach your child how to hide using camouflage.

Photo courtesy of www.pixabay.com

This topic is of great interest to me personally and one in which I am uniquely qualified as a subject matter expert. With three published books on camouflage and concealment, it is no surprise that my children already have a solid foundation on this topic. Both of my children knew what a ghillie suit and camouflage was long before they could spell either word.

Even when they could not wear camouflage clothing out of practicality or personal preference, they still knew how to obscure the physical outline of their body and cover up bright colors. I find this more challenging with girls, as my girls have a decidedly biased preference to pinks, purples, and blues. Because camouflage is deeply associated with hunting and the military, it seems natural for boys to show an affinity towards it based on long-held societal norms.

While I may not be able to influence their daily fashion choices, I know that in the event of having to make a bug-out escape to a secluded rural area, the girls know when they need to suit up in an appropriate camouflage pattern or muted color scheme. Despite their early childhood fascination with dirt and mud, I doubt they will apply mud to their hands and face with the same reckless abandon of their toddler years.

Record the physical features and personality traits of your child.

Photo courtesy of www.pixabay.com

Nobody knows your child as you do. Inasmuch, you have a tremendous advantage to have access to information about your children that no one else does or should have, with the exception perhaps of your family physician.

In the event your child becomes lost or separated, having the most detailed description of your child for the police and investigators is an absolute necessity. Birthmarks are key descriptor used to isolate and narrow down the identity of a missing person. Common birthmarks are moles and melanin anomalies that are either darker or lighter than the surrounding skin. Other types of distinguishing marks or features can include scars from previous injuries or surgical procedures.

Knowing the most current physical characteristics of your child like height, weight, hair and eye color would seem pointless to record, as most would assume a parent would automatically know these things. However, one would be surprised to learn that the stress over a lost child might short-circuit someone's memory. It is also a wise idea to find out your child's blood type and Rhesus (Rh) factor.

Just like physical features, your child's personality is also unique. While it takes time for their personalities to develop fully, there will be key features that should be recognized with relative ease. Most parents will gladly attest to a child's strong-willed tendencies or shyness around people. Parents also describe how their children handle conflict and solve problems, the child's adapting and overcoming mechanisms, or how the child behaves when tired. All of these factors become important when search and rescue personnel attempt to reunite children to their parents.

Teach your child about land navigation, orienteering, and map reading.

Photo courtesy of www.pixabay.com

People, including and especially children, like to know where they are. No one likes being lost or lacking a sense of direction or purpose in life. Many of the life goals we set for ourselves require a clear, logical navigational path offering step-by-step guidance for the accomplishment and attainment of those goals.

The easiest way to begin teaching children about navigation is by taking them places that are large enough to require a site map in order to find and visit all of the exhibits. The local zoo is the perfect example and is a location that is suited for teaching other skills within this guide. The maps are often colorful as to attract and keep a child's attention. They are also pictograph-based, meaning they use pictures to describe where certain exhibits and attractions are. These types of maps also include a legend containing symbols to identify toilet facilities, food courts, information booths, and souvenir shops.

As the child grows older, having them find and locate cities and destinations on a road map instills confidence in the child. Adding to the fact that they are assisting in preventing the family from becoming lost along the way gives the child a greater sense of responsibility and accomplishment when you have reached your desired destination. I can remember as a child being able to memorize the route to take to the grocery store, the bank, the doctor's office, etc. and recalling the street names. This served me well after I received my driver's license. I was able to find most places without asking the location.

Teach your child how to build emergency survival shelters.

Photo courtesy of www.pixabay.com

Survival experts and instructors often state that shelter building is one of the most crucial survival skills. Without adequate shelter from the elements, core body temperature can decrease rapidly in inclement weather from a matter of hours all the way down to several minutes. The colder the outside temperature, the more important this becomes.

Having your child learn some basic sheltering techniques can mean the difference between life and death. There are plenty of online resources, as well as training videos on YouTube explaining how to erect simple shelters. I observed my girls when they were four years old building a lean-to shelter unassisted after watching a Curious George video. They would spend hours outside building numerous shelters with whatever items they could find. This developed their love of a various range of survival skills.

On one particular YouTube channel, *Survival Lily*, hosted by a woman from Austria was, and still is, a great influence on my girls. Seeing a woman demonstrating the skills and performing the tasks provided the added inspiration and empowerment to our girls.

Teach your child how to build fires using various ignition methods.

Photo courtesy of www.pixabay.com

Typically, as parents, we do not want our children to play with fire. Nevertheless, as children get older and their natural curiosity begins developing, introducing them to the principles of fire science and combustion methods is a great way to balance that curiosity with practicality.

Children oftentimes will want to participate in fire lighting activities earlier than they can be deemed responsible to do so. However, with careful adult supervision and proper safeguards in place, children can begin learning these skills as early as five years of age.

It should be noted that focusing first on the more primitive fire-starting methods might reduce a child's ability to produce a spark or ember, thus igniting any potential fire fuel. However, the child's persistence will eventually be rewarded and a skill that is even hard for some adults to accomplish with consistent success will be learned.

When we lived in Washington, our girls became quite proficient with a ferrocerium rod. They also learned how to make fire with a magnifying glass, as well as other more conventional methods.   With the proper supervision, they neither burned themselves nor burned down any structures or wooded areas.

Teach your child how to procure, filter, and purify water for drinking.

Photo courtesy of www.pixabay.com

Water is essential to all life on planet Earth. Clean water is vital for survival. However, finding and procuring clean water can be difficult for urban dwellers that are dependent exclusively on city water systems and purchased bottled water.

Water is procurable from a number of sources; however, rainwater is most likely and safest alternate source in an urban environment. Brainstorm with your child the materials needed for water collection and potential water sources in your area. Some inner-city parks have featured fountains or ponds. Maybe there is a toddler splash pad or a freshwater stream or lake close to where you live. Researching the nearby water sources will help determine any additional steps are required to make the water safe to drink.

The next important step is teaching your child about the different methods of water treatment. This also provides a great opportunity to teach children about microbiology, pathogens, disease, bacteria and viruses, etc. Boiling questionable water is the most common method of making water potable or safe to drink.

Instructing your child on different filtration methods prior to boiling will help the water look a lot better prior to drinking. Something as simple as a bandana or a T-shirt can help reduce the amount of sediment and noticeable contaminants.   More elaborate methods that contain gravel, sand, and charcoal can be constructed to filter water as well.

Teach your child about the importance and benefits of physical fitness.

Photo courtesy of www.pixabay.com

This is one area that many parents have become slack for two reasons: their own lack of personal fitness and the over-reliance on electronic entertainment. While I can say I have succeeded in limiting the entertainment aspect, I have failed in the other. That failure not only affects my overall health, but it sets the poor example for my children, as they grow older. In the child's eyes, they may see a parent who does not value their health, and as a result, may choose to place a lower value or sense of importance on physical health.

There exist multitudes of reports and studies justifying the benefits of daily exercise and proper diet, which I do not feel the need to repeat. Suffice it to say, the benefits severely outweigh (pun intended) the alternatives. Maintaining a healthy weight, core strength, and cardiovascular health are just a few of the reasons why physical fitness is important.

Team sports may also help develop interpersonal communication skills, conflict resolution, problem solving, and of course, team work. Working towards and achieving a common goal will serve your child well as they prepare for future endeavors in the job market, as well as their personal relationships.

Teach your child how to handle, carry, and use a pocketknife.

Photo courtesy of www.pixabay.com

A pocketknife is a useful tool. It is also a convention in the passage of manhood. In some societies and cultures, the presentation of a knife to an older child or young adult is an acknowledgement of the greater responsibility (both familial and societal) to assist in adult tasks. It really does not matter whether you have boys or girls; the tool is equally useful, regardless of the gender of the person wielding it. Despite its intended purpose to cut things, it should not be viewed as an object to fear when used or handled correctly. The main thing is to provide proper instruction and safe technique when teaching your child how to use and carry a pocketknife.

In addition to how to carry and use a pocketknife, it is also important to instruct children regarding the "when" as well. Most schools now have a zero tolerance policy pertaining to weapons of any kind. This often includes pocketknives, regardless of size or intended purpose. As such, any presentation or gifting of a knife should include a very somber conversation regarding when and how the child is to have the knife in their possession.

There is nothing wrong with further stipulation of use only with adult supervision or in the context of outdoor survival skills. Those boundaries are up to the parent or guardian to set as they deem them appropriate.

Furthermore, the added responsibility of maintaining a pocketknife through regular sharpening and inspection teaches the child proper tool upkeep. This keeps the child from developing a negligent or flippant attitude and disregard for tools and other possessions requiring regular care and maintenance.

Teach your child how to grow and forage/find food.

Photo courtesy of www.pixabay.com

Young children love exploring. They also have the built-in instinct to find things to put in their mouths. As they begin to explore outdoors, they will become aware of different plants that have the potential to serve as food. Growing vegetables and herbs in a garden or maintaining fruit/nut trees is an excellent way to teach children about food production in a controlled environment. Children love to eat the fruits of their labor and are often excited about the contributions they make while planting, weeding, and harvesting their crops.

One of the highlights of the summer is finding a wild blackberry patch and gorging oneself on the sweet berries. My children seemed to eat them faster than I could pick them when they were toddlers.

As they get older, you can begin to introduce the concept of foraging and plant identification (discussed in the next chapter). This also serves a greater purpose to alleviate potential fear of starvation should the child become lost in a survival situation. Likewise, it can help the child identify potential medicinal plants that, while unable to be used as food, still may be of some benefit.

Foraging is not without its potential dangers regarding poisonous foods, such as hawthorn berries or the numerous varieties of poisonous mushrooms. There is also the possibility of encountering wild animals feeding on a shared food source. Therefore, caution should be taken to ensure animals are given a wide berth and not encroach on their territory while feeding.

Teach your child plant identification.

Photo courtesy of www.pixabay.com

Few things can save your child more effectively than basic plant identification. Anyone who has ever been exposed to poison ivy is probably able to immediately identify it for the rest of his or her life. It is not a pleasant experience. Likewise, the ability to recognize other poisonous or noxious vegetation (or their fruit, pods, or seeds) can save your child from emergency room visits and even death.

Many times, plants can be merely minor skin irritants, while others produce welts like stinging nettles and blisters like the aforementioned poison ivy and sumac. Teaching your child how to recognize the difference from edible plants and non-edible plants goes back to skills they can learn in the Scouts programs.

Knowing the various plants in your region will go a long way as to helping identify both beneficial and poisonous plants. It is also helpful to learn the safe handling/harvesting techniques for plants that are beneficial, but still potentially irritating. Stinging nettles is a prime example. The leaves and roots are often used as an ingredient for an herbal tea, but the leaves and stems produce painful welts when touched with bare hands.

Teach your child animal identification.

Photo courtesy of www.pixabay.com

As mentioned back in the foraging chapter, many animals eat the same foods as humans. Omnivores, such as black bears, are known for their wide diet range. Among one of their favorites is blueberries. Humans like blueberries as well, but competition over a food source is ultimately going to go in the black bear's favor, as far as wild foraging is concerned.

I have found some of my most memorable childhood and adult experiences have been encountering and observing wildlife. To me, there is very little else, that is as serene and peaceful as watching a mother with her offspring, the ingenuity of animal hunting or gathering food, or the battle over breeding status. There is a profound sense of gratitude being fortunate to observe the animal world going about its existence without any interference from humans. I can sit and watch for hours or until the animals move along out of sight.

With that being said, being able to identify the various animal species within an area can help your child determine what animals can help warn of danger, which animals qualify as food, and which animals have the potential to attack and become a greater danger when alerted to human presence. Most animals attempt to avoid human contact. Surprised, cornered, or wounded animals are more likely to become aggressive, charging or attacking to protect either offspring or territory or both.

Teach your child how to swim.

Photo courtesy of www.pixabay.com

Every year, hundreds of children die from accidental drowning. While there are certain circumstances that contribute to a tragic ending, most are the results of unsupervised negligence on behalf of the parent/guardian and the child not having learned how to swim. The child need not have Olympic swimming ability, but should be able to tread water, doggie paddle, or swim 25-50 meters.

In addition to the lifesaving component of having the ability to swim, it helps alleviate the fear of water and gives the child the confidence to participate in many water-based activities where swimming is an obvious prerequisite safety measure.

I am not a particularly strong swimmer, but in an effort to develop core body strength, utilize low-impact cardiovascular exercise, and increase family time with a shared activity, we decided to visit a local pool every two weeks. This focused activity has and will continue to increase swimming skills for the entire family.

It would also be of benefit to learn some basic water rescue techniques involving the use of life rings, poles, and hooks. Some water situations are too dangerous to enter the water to rescue someone else, but having the basic knowledge to perform a water rescue will help your child provide necessary assistance should the occasion present itself.

Teach your child how to predict weather using clouds and animal behavior.

Photo courtesy of www.pixabay.com

When I was a kid growing up in Illinois, my brothers and neighbors were outside playing anytime the sun was out. Most of the neighbor kids were farm kids and had chores to complete. During the summer months, we baled hay and straw with them. We would use our eyes, ears, and nose to notice changes in the weather. We learned about the different cloud types and formations in school by name, but we learned their characteristics out in the fields. We could smell the ground being disked a mile away and we could smell the rain just before the first drops hit the ground. We could hear insect chatter increase before the rain and intensify at dusk. The color of the sky would tell how fast we needed to get out of the field, off equipment and hills, and seek shelter in the basement.

Growing up in a rural community, we found ourselves surrounded by farmers. We often assisted with our friends' chores in order to speed up the process so we could play sooner. Cattle and horses seemed to know when storms were brewing. Flies and other biting insects would become more active, which in turn, prompted the barn swallows to come out and feast. Chickens would scurry into the coups and the outside dogs would head for the open barns or doghouse. Other animals, including the wild ones, would find a place to bed down and take shelter just before the storms would hit.

This basic, easy-to-learn skill does not cost any money to learn or put into practice. Besides, being outdoors gives one little excuse or reason to complain about the classroom. It can save your child from being caught in rainstorms or other inclement weather conditions. However, it may not keep your child out of rain puddles and mud holes.

Teach your child about the importance of sanitation and personal hygiene.

Photo courtesy of www.pixabay.com

Hygiene and sanitation are among the first things most parents train their children to practice. It often starts simultaneously with toilet training. By reinforcing proper hygiene practices, it reduces the spread of disease, reduces the risk of infections and contracting viruses.

As this book was being finalized, the world was experiencing the viral pandemic known as COVID-19. Early on, it was determined that good hygiene and sanitation guidelines would help slow the transmission rate. The worldwide result was a renewed public relations campaign for proper hand-washing techniques, as we as good hygiene etiquette for covering coughs and sneezes, staying home when ill, socially distancing from others to stay out of droplet range.

Whether virus outbreaks or pandemic scares demand basic hygiene protocols, teaching your child proper personal hygiene and cleanliness guidelines will keep your child safer and healthier. This topic also migrates into household cleanliness (the never-ending, messy child's bedroom), and kitchen and bathroom sanitizing methods. Here again, children learn better by doing and participating in the cleaning process.

Teach your child how to cache and use survival items.

Photo courtesy of www.pixabay.com

Teaching your child how to use survival tools and how to cache them effectively for use during wilderness emergencies is vital. Having a few essential items stashed away at a familiar location out of the elements is a smart plan, should your child be caught in an unexpected storm or a passing rain shower. The items do not need to be expensive or extravagant; they just need to function well and be easy to use.

I enjoyed this activity immensely because I felt I was hiding something. My friends and I would hide things in hollowed out trees, suspended from upper tree limbs, under bridges, or buried underground. I started out using inexpensive things to make sure the contents were protected from water damage or incidental discovery. Over time, as my skills increased, I utilized better camouflaging and waterproofing methods that I could justify hiding items of greater monetary and sentimental value.

This skill can also foster the opposite in learning about discovery methods using activities such as geocaching and metal detecting. Investigative skills such as deductive reasoning and logic play an integral part in the use and application of many cache methods. The metal detecting aspect has some income-generating potential that also may be an incentive for children.

Teach your child how to avoid dangerous situations.

Photo courtesy of www.pixabay.com

A majority of maintaining safety and well-being is related directly to how effectively and correctly, we perceive and identify hazardous situations. It is my hope throughout this brief guide that the readers are informed about the many dangers in the world and they will make wise, practical, and informed decisions on how best to mitigate the risks our children may encounter. Parents are the key teachers and instructors of their children and must prepare them with the necessary tools to adapt and overcome these dangers.

As humans, we can rely on instinct, intuition, experience, and acquired knowledge. Teaching our children using these things will better prepare them to avoid danger and survive the dangerous situations that sometimes cannot be avoided.

This guide does not and cannot address every possible situation or scenario a child may encounter or be unwillingly subjected. The learning and practical application of the suggested skills contained within will help protect your children, guide them into productive adulthood, and sustain/maintain them throughout their lives. May God watch over and protect you and your family.

ABOUT THE AUTHOR

Matthew Dermody is the author of several other books ranging in topics from camouflage and concealment to personal safety and threat detection. He currently lives in Australia with his wife and their twin daughters.

www.ingramcontent.com/pod-product-compliance
Lightning Source LLC
Chambersburg PA
CBHW061723250726
48657CB00002B/740